MW01133284

"WHEN I CONSIDER YOUR
HEAVENS, THE WORK OF
YOUR FINGERS, THE MOON
AND THE STARS,
WHICH YOU HAVE SET
IN PLACE, WHAT IS
MANKIND THAT YOU ARE
MINDFUL OF THEM,
HUMAN BEINGS THAT YOU
CARE FOR THEM?"

— PSALMS 8:3-4

GOD IS BIGGER

FOR GOD,
I PRAY THAT I WILL
NEVER FORGET JUST
HOW BIG YOU ARE ♡

GOD IS BIGGER

By Jess Elford

HOW BIG
IS GOD?

GOD IS
BIGGER
THAN ME

GOD IS
BIGGER
THAN AN
ELEPHANT

GOD IS
GREATER
THAN THE
DESERT

GOD IS
WIDER
THAN THE
SEA

GOD IS
HIGHER
THAN A
MOUNTAIN

GOD IS
LARGER
THAN THE
EARTH

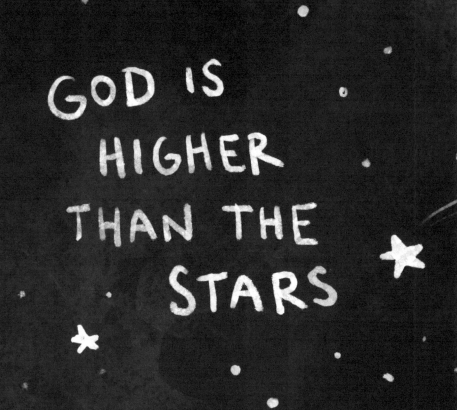

GOD IS
BIGGER
THAN THE
WHOLE...

UNIVERSE!!

SO WHEN MY
WORRIES
   FEEL TOO BIG,

I DON'T NEED
   TO BE AFRAID...

BECAUSE NO MATTER

HOW BIG MY WORRIES ARE...

MY GOD IS
BIGGER
_____
IN EVERY
WAY

Jess Elford is an author & illustrator (and cinnamon toast enthusiast!) from rural Queensland, Australia. Before graduating from the design program at the Queensland College of Art, Jess had already illustrated multiple children's books (her first when she was just 14 years old!) Jess is also an avid traveller and dream-chaser and has worked in some really magical places like Walt Disney World in Florida, USA as well as around the world on cruise ships.

@ thosepencilshavings • thosepencilshavings@gmail.com • Those Pencil Shavings

Printed in the USA
CPSIA information can be obtained
at www.ICGtesting.com
LVHW062124010224
770657LV00015B/207